easy

Parakeet
Care

Nikki Moustaki

T.F.H. Publications
One TFH Plaza
Third and Union Avenues
Neptune City, NJ 07753

This book has been published with the intent to provide accurate and authoritative information in regard to the subject matter within. While every precaution has been taken in preparation of this book, the publisher and author assume no responsibili-ty for errors or omissions. Neither is any liability assumed for damages resulting from the use of the information herein.

If you purchased this book without a cover you should be aware that this book is stolen. It was reported as unsold and destroyed to the publisher and neither the author nor the publisher has received any payment for this "stripped book."

Library of Congress Cataloging-in-Publication Data
Moustaki, Nikki, 1970-
Quick & easy parakeet care / Nikki Moustaki.
p. cm.
Includes index.
ISBN 0-7938-1019-1 (alk. paper)
1.Budgerigar. I. Title: Quick and easy parakeet care. II. Title.
SF473.B8M68 2004
636.6'864–dc22
2004008780

www.tfh.com

Distributed by T.F.H. Publications, Inc.
Neptune City, NJ

Table of Contents

You and Your Parakeet

Congratulations on your decision to bring home a parakeet! You're in popular company. Parakeets (called budgies in most countries) are the most widely kept companion bird in the world. Parakeets make affectionate companions and bond readily to humans who are patient and kind to their birds.

If you want your parakeet to be an affectionate companion, it's best to have just one, as long as you are able to pay a lot of attention to him. If you have less time to spend with your pet, you might want to consider obtaining a pair of parakeets. This way, your birds will keep themselves entertained and occupied, and you won't have to worry about your companion alone at home pining away for you.

Parakeet Origins

The parakeet's scientific name is *Melopsittacus undulates*; roughly translated, it means "song bird with wavy lines." The word "budgie" comes from the Aboriginal Australians' word for this bird, betchegara (budgerigar) which means "good to eat." Parakeets are originally from the Australian outback, but your parakeet was bred in your country of origin, not imported from the wild. The parakeet is prolific in captivity and has been bred for hundreds of years.

Most of the parakeets you see in pet shops are small birds, but others look rather large—those are the English budgies. Even though English budgies are often more expensive and shorter lived, they make just as good companions as "regular" budgies. These bigger budgies are the result of selective breeding and do not occur in the wild.

Things to Consider Before Getting a Parakeet

Parakeets are wonderful family companions and are able to love multiple members of the family. A parakeet that is a family companion should get a lot of attention and care—there might be multiple members of the family looking out for the bird's well-being, and that can only be a good thing. Do your homework and find out what parakeet ownership is all about. Then, if you still want the companionship of this little bird, go for it!

Parakeet Lifespan

A parakeet can live to be 12 to 15 years old with the appropriate care and a healthy diet, though the larger English budgie only lives to be about 7 or 8 years of age.

Expenses

Parakeets are not, as a general rule, very expensive birds to keep. The first expense you will incur is the parakeet himself, plus all of the other add-ons that you'll need to get started, such as an adequate cage, cups, toys, food, and a play gym.

You'll also have the necessary expense of a yearly visit to the avian veterinarian for a well-bird checkup. Once your avian veterinarian gets to know your bird, he or she will be better able to take care of him in the event of an accident or illness.

One responsibility of parakeet ownership is to give your bird safe playtime outside of his cage every day.

In addition to these costs, keep in mind that you may want to splurge now and then on extra toys or treats, which will bring the total expense higher.

Responsibilities of Parakeet Ownership

Your parakeet relies on you for all of his needs, which include proper housing, feeding and nutrition, playtime out of the cage, and overall safety. You are responsible for every aspect of your parakeet's life.

Here's a short list of responsibilities you take on when you get a parakeet:

• Daily cleaning of the cage
• Weekly thorough cleaning of the cage and the surrounding area
• Offering fresh water twice a day

- Offering and changing fresh foods daily
- Having safe playtime out of the cage daily
- Watching closely for signs of illness and taking your parakeet to the veterinarian in the event of an accident or if you suspect something is wrong
- Parakeet-proofing your home so that it is a safe place for him to play
- Watching other pets closely when the bird is out of his cage
- Making sure the cage is kept out of drafts and that the cage is kept in a room that doesn't get too cold or too warm
- Checking the bird's cage and toys daily for dangerous wear and tear

Choosing the Right Parakeet for You

If you decide that you can handle the responsibilities that come with owning a parakeet as a pet, you are ready for the next step: choosing the right parakeet for you.

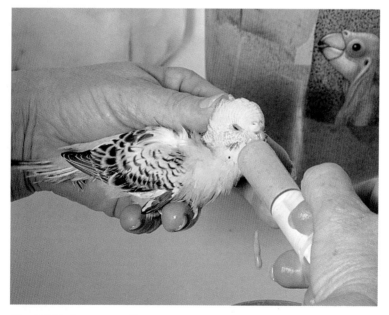

Hand-fed babies are usually very easy to tame and have friendly temperaments.

Quick & Easy Parakeet Care

Age

If you want your parakeet to be tame, the best choice for you is a fledgling. A fledgling is a young bird that has just come out of the nest and is able to eat on his own. Most baby parakeets are eating on their own at six to eight weeks of age and can be taken to a new home at that time. Some breeders might want to wait a little longer before they sell the babies to make certain that they are strong and healthy.

Male and female parakeets are easily distinguished by the colors of their ceres once they are mature, but both sexes make equally good companions.

An adult bird that has already been tamed also makes a great companion. Parakeets reach young adulthood at six to nine months of age. If you get an adult bird that has never been handled by humans before, you will have to spend more time taming him.

If you want a really tame, sweet baby, try to find a breeder that hand-feeds babies. This means that the breeder takes the baby away from his parents when he is still reliant upon them and takes over the parental duties. As a result, the baby parakeet will become very tame because he is used to being handled.

Quality Time

Expect to spend at least two hours a day with your bird and more on the days when you have more time. That's a commitment of at least 14 hours a week. Be sure you set aside time each day to socialize and visit with your bird.

Chatterboxes

Parakeets are among the best talkers of the commonly kept companion birds, with some individuals having been reported as saying hundreds of words and phrases.

Male or Female?

Parakeets are a dimorphic species, which means that there's a visual difference between the sexes. A mature male parakeet has a dark blue cere (the fleshy part just above his nostrils), and a mature female has a pink or darkish-brown cere. Both sexes make equally good pets.

Two parakeets, especially a male and a female, will be quite content together. A single parakeet can be happy, too, but will become lonely if left alone too often. Spend time with your bird every day.

Color

Parakeets come in more than 70 color variations, and more are

Though the wild budgie is green, domestic parakeets now come in more than 70 color variations.

Quick & Easy Parakeet Care

being developed each year. Even so, you will probably only find about ten distinct colors in your local pet shop. There is no difference in the pet quality among the different colors. Blue, green, yellow, white—the birds are all the same.

The wild budgie is green, and that is the base color from which all of the other colors were developed. Those other colors are called "mutations" and are a natural occurrence in nature; budgie breeders capitalized on this fact by breeding those mutated birds to one another, creating a wide variety of colors.

The feathers on a healthy parakeet will appear tight, shiny, and flat against the body.

Finding a Healthy Parakeet

Once you've decided on the age, sex, and color of your parakeet, you now have to make sure that you choose a healthy one. It is important to take your parakeet to an avian veterinarian for a well-bird checkup appointment within three days of bringing your new

Parakeet Intelligence

For having such a tiny skull, the parakeet is no birdbrain. This little bird is highly intelligent, able to recognize the people and things in his life. Each parakeet is an individual with his own tastes and ideas about things. Occasionally, you can convince a parakeet of something (such as convincing him to eat a certain food), but there are other things he will decide for himself (such as when it's the right time to take a bath).

bird home, but there are several initial things you can look for yourself to make sure your parakeet is healthy.

Eyes

A parakeet's eyes should be round, clear, and bright. There should be no crust or discharge from the eyes. Eyes should show an attitude of alertness.

Nares and Cere

A parakeet's nostrils are called nares, and they are located on the cere, which is the fleshy part just above the beak. The nares should be clean and without discharge. The cere should not be crusty or peeling.

Feathers

The feathers of a healthy parakeet are shiny and tight, laying flat against the body. A parakeet with excessively ruffled feathers or bald patches may be ill. The exception to this is the crested budgie, which has a crest of raised feathers on the top of his head. The other exception is the feather duster budgie, which has excessively long feathers, though it is unlikely that you will easily find one of these birds for sale.

Feet

A parakeet's feet should be free of debris. The parakeet should be able to perch easily on both feet. Sometimes a parakeet becomes crippled in the nest and can have splayed legs or other foot problems—this is no reason to turn him away. A crippled parakeet still has his wings and will be able to get around if allowed full flight.

Vent

The vent is underneath the bird and is the place where waste is eliminated. The vent should be clean and not crusted with wastes or other material.

Quick & Easy Parakeet Care

Attitude

A healthy parakeet is active, chattery, and always on the move. A fluffed, sleepy-looking parakeet that is sitting on the bottom of the cage might be ill. Try to choose a parakeet that is wandering around the cage socializing, eating, and bathing—this bird is active and alert and eager to go home with a new, loving owner.

Where to Find the Right Parakeet

There are several possible sources for you to obtain a parakeet as a companion, including breeders, pet shops, bird specialty shops, and adoption centers.

Parakeet Breeders

One way to find an English budgie is through a parakeet breeder, someone who breeds for mutations and for showing. Most breeders are serious about the hobby and can help you to find the best parakeet for you. Many will also provide references that you can contact, so you can be assured of the quality of the breeder's birds. Make sure you request a health guarantee and the right to return

It's best to choose a parakeet that is active, chattery, and energetic—these are all signs of good health and attitude.

your parakeet should he not get a clean bill of health from your avian veterinarian.

Pet Shops and Bird Specialty Shops

Your local pet shop or bird specialty shop is another source and will often have a cage full of parakeets, all ready to go home with you. Look for a shop where the employees seem to know about birds and will take the time to help you and answer your questions. Make sure the birds appear well cared for and healthy and as always, ask for a health guarantee with the bird you choose.

Adoption as an Option

How about adopting a parakeet? Statistically, birds stay in the average home for two years. That's not very long, considering this time is only a small percentage of a parakeet's lifespan.

Think about giving a home to a rescued parakeet. Just because the bird is not a baby does not mean that he will not come to see you as his best friend.

Call your local animal shelter, bird club, or budgie society, and put your name on the list of potential homes for unwanted parakeets. The parakeet that you get from the shelter may have health issues to resolve and may have some behavioral issues as well. If you can deal with some initial challenges, a rescued bird can make a great companion.

Housing Your Parakeet

As you've probably noticed when visiting pet shops or your favorite pet retailer, there are many different types of birdcages on the market. Some of them are even labeled "parakeet cages." But which one should you buy?

There are several factors to consider in order to purchase the right cage for your parakeet. Remember, the cage you choose will be your feathered pal's home, not his prison. It will be the place where he will spend considerable time, and he needs a place to rest, eat, and play.

Bigger is Better

A parakeet's cage should be as large and as roomy as possible. Make sure the cage is big enough to accommodate perches, food dishes, and toys, while still allowing your bird enough space for flying.

Cage Size

Some cages are labeled "parakeet" cages—these are usually small, pastel-colored cages that are geared toward children. This is an unacceptable home for your parakeet unless your bird is out of his cage and interacting with you for most of the day. In any other case, you should buy a larger cage. A cage that is designated to be large enough for a few budgies is the best size to purchase, even if you only have one parakeet. Your bird will appreciate the extra room.

When you find a large cage that will give your parakeet plenty of room, make certain that the bars of the cage are not wide enough for the bird to stick his head through—this can be extremely dangerous.

Square or rectangular cages are best because the corners offer security and the shape adds more cage space.

Offer your parakeet a number of perches that vary in size, shape, and material.

Cage Shape

Square or rectangular cages are far better than round cages. Corners will make your parakeet feel more secure, and a round cage does not offer that comfort. Square or rectangular cages also offer more cage space for the same basic cage size.

Cage Materials

Most cages are made of metal and plastic, and some are coated to add a color or a texture. Be careful that the coating on the outside of the cage is nontoxic and won't harm your birds. If you notice that your parakeet picks away at the coating, remove the bird from the

Safety First

The best materials for a parakeet cage are safe metals and hard plastics. Wooden and antique cages can be dangerous because they are easily destroyed, can harbor bacteria, and may contain toxins.

cage immediately and get a new cage that does not have a coating. Ingestion of this coating can be deadly.

Consider practicality and comfort when you are looking at cages and evaluate the cosmetics of the cage last. A "pretty" cage is not always the best or safest cage for your parakeet. Some decorative cages have metal scrollwork that can catch a toe and cause bleeding. This can be dangerous for a parakeet.

Many cages open from the bottom and have "guillotine" style doors that can snap down and injure your bird. It's better to find a cage with doors that open from the side, like the door to a house, or doors that open from the top and pull downward. If you already have a cage with the "guillotine" style doors, invest in inexpensive spring clips from the hardware store, which will prevent the door from inadvertently slamming shut and harming your bird.

Wooden cages are unacceptable for parakeets because they easily harbor harmful bacteria and toxins—stick with safe metals and plastics.

Cage Accessories
There are several cage accessories that you must have in order to keep your parakeet happy and healthy. Cage accessories are a non-negotiable part of owning a parakeet.

Perches
The cage may have come with a few plastic perches or maybe even a couple of wooden dowels. While they are decent perches, these alone don't provide an adequate selection. Because your parakeet uses his feet so much, it's important that he has as many different perch widths, materials, and textures to stand on as possible. If your bird only has one type and size of perch to stand on, he can develop serious foot problems.

Food and Water Dishes

The cage you purchased probably came with a couple of cups for seed and water, which is a good start, but you'll need a few more cups to complete your set, including other types of cups for different food items. You will need at least one cup for food, one for water, and one for fresh foods, such as fruits and vegetables.

Plastic is not the finest material for a bird cup. The plastic can become scratched and hold bacteria in the grooves of the scratches. Stainless steel is a great material for bird cups. It's durable and easy to clean. Ceramic cups are also a good choice. Both of these types of cups can be found with holders that keep them secure in the cage to avoid seed dumping.

To keep your parakeet's cage clean and to save valuable time, keep two sets of dishes. You will have six dishes—two for seed/pellets, two for water, and two for fresh foods. Each day, remove the dirty dishes and replace them with the clean ones. This will allow you to disinfect the other dishes for the next day.

Tube-style waterers are popular among parakeet owners because the water often stays cleaner longer in the tube—there is less area for the parakeet to toss food and droppings into. However, just because the water lasts longer doesn't mean that you don't have to change it every day.

Millet Holders and Birdy Kabobs

A millet holder is a good, inexpensive investment—this little clip allows you to attach the millet spray to the side of the cage where your bird can "work" at it.

A "birdy kabob" is also a great way to get your little feathered pal to eat his greens. Simply thread the fruits and vegetables onto the kabob and hang it in the cage. This gives your parakeet the feeling of having to "work" for his food, something he would do in the wild.

Be careful if you decide to use tube-style feeders. Parakeets hull their seeds, and it may look like they are getting plenty of seed when in reality they only have access to the hulls. Make sure to add fresh seed to the tube every day.

Mineral Blocks and Cuttlebones

A mineral block and a beak block are essentially the same thing—a lump of minerals shaped into a block or a fruit or vegetable shape. Your parakeet will appreciate this treat, and it will help to keep his beak trim. It will also add some calcium to his diet. Another common accessory, the cuttlebone, comes from the cuttlefish. This is an important cage accessory, not just because your parakeet will enjoy working on it, but because it is a good source of calcium as well.

Cage Covers

Some parakeets like their cage to be completely covered at night, while others may only want to be covered halfway or on three sides. Covering the cage offers the bird a degree of security and protection. Your bird will not be disturbed from sleep by light in the house or a cat slinking around. The cover will protect the bird from drafts, and the dark cage may allow you more sleeping time if your bird likes to get up with the sun. Offering a cover is like tucking your birds in at night.

Covering the Cage

Some parakeets like to be covered at night, though some others become frightened in the dark. A cover can help to eliminate nighttime drafts and will allow the bird to sleep longer in the morning.

Parakeets love swings and will get a good amount of exercise with these enjoyable toys.

Toys

Toys are extremely important to the health and well-being of a single parakeet. Toys are going to make up the majority of your parakeet's "job." Wild parakeets work all day at finding food and water and staying safe. Your domestic parakeet doesn't get nearly this much exercise, though he does require it. Toys are for chewing, flinging, preening, and arguing with. A beloved toy can offer a lonely budgie a sense of comfort and a sense of home.

Parakeets love shiny, interactive toys that they can fling around or show affection to. You may have noticed that some toys for budgies are directed toward alleviating loneliness, such as mirror toys, floss and preening toys, or toys shaped like another life-sized budgie.

Parakeets are destructive, but they are not incredibly powerful, which is why there are many plastic toys on the market geared toward them. Consider a mixture of wooden, rope, and plastic toys. Parakeets love swings, so don't scrimp in the swing department.

Toy Safety

Not all toys are safe for your parakeet. Remember, he has a very tiny head that can get caught in a ring, or he could catch his toes in odd places, such as the slots in a jingle bell. Old toys with sharp corners or fraying rope can be dangerous as well. File sharp corners with a nail file and trim any loose strings that could potentially get wrapped around a neck or a foot.

Mirror toys are popular for the single parakeet. Though they are fun and interactive, your parakeet may become so enamored of his reflection that he forgets about you and about his training. If you notice that your bird is becoming too affectionate with his mirror, you might want to remove it temporarily until some of the bird's affections return to you.

Play gyms are not only wonderful accessories for your parakeet, but they also serve as training tools.

Playtime

Toys are very important for parakeets, especially a bird that is kept alone. Mirror toys and bells are particularly appreciated. Inspect all toys and make sure they are safe before you give them to your bird.

Play Gyms

A play gym usually consists of a platform to which perches, ladders, and toys are affixed. It will give your bird an opportunity to play and get some much-needed activity. A play gym is also a great training tool because you can place the bird on the steady perch and work with him there, rather than trying to work with him close to his cage, where he might seek refuge.

Bird Baths

Bathing is good for your parakeet's skin and is a natural behavior—even though it might get a bit messy. Preventing your bird from bathing is a terrible idea, as is forcing your bird to bathe. Your bird knows when it's time for a bath, and he will do it in his own time. Most birds bathe in their water dish, so be sure you clean it often. You can provide your parakeet with a separate bath that he may prefer to the water dish. Your local pet supply store will have several different sizes and types of birdbaths available.

Alternative Housing

It's kind of silly to call any bird a "cage bird." Birds aren't really meant to be kept in cages, and that's something often missed in any discussion of bird keeping. There's often a lot of emphasis placed on how to keep the bird in such a manner that it makes us happy or is easiest for us, without giving much consideration to the fact that the bird probably just wants to do what comes naturally—flying.

This is not to say that you should let your parakeet fly around your home. There are plenty of dangers a parakeet can get into inside the

The More the Merrier

Parakeets are generally peaceful birds and do well in an aviary setting. They can be kept with cockatiels and non-aggressive softbills as well.

average home, not to mention that he could escape through an open door or window.

Aviaries

One solution is to purchase an aviary, a very large cage that houses one or more parakeets. Some are large enough to hold an entire flock. (Parakeets are flocking animals and enjoy one another's company if there is ample room.)

You can create an aviary in your backyard or in your living room. You can also order an aviary from a bird supply catalogue or buy one from a larger bird specialty pet shop. An aviary should be at least large enough to fit a human adult inside of it.

Parakeet Habitats

A habitat is an aviary taken to the next level. It is usually larger than an aviary and contains natural elements, such as plants and running water. Some zoos have habitats, and they are also becoming popular with bird fanciers. The idea of a habitat is to recreate, as closely as possible, the animal's natural environment. Although it would be quite difficult to recreate the Australian grasslands, allowing your parakeets to fly and interact with nature is a start. Because most habitats are kept outside, there are considerations, such as predators and foul weather, to contend with, but a well-built and well-planned habitat can withstand such odds.

Parakeet Nutrition

The trick to feeding your parakeet properly can be summed up in one word: variety. Parakeets are prone to all kinds of nutritional disorders. They are notorious for becoming overweight and will gorge on seed to the exclusion of just about everything else if you let them. Obesity is a major health issue for parakeets, so it's important to take extra care and ensure that your bird gets the proper nutrition he needs to live out his entire lifespan in good health. No bird can live well on seed alone.

A Parakeet's Basic Diet

A fresh, healthful diet is the key to the longevity of your parakeet. You won't be able to mimic a wild parakeet's diet, but you may be

A healthy, balanced diet is the key to the longevity of your parakeet.

able to come close enough to keep your parakeet happy and in prime condition. The basic elements of a parakeet's diet include water, seeds, pellets, fruits, vegetables, and even table foods.

The Importance of Water

Life can't exist without water, and neither can your parakeet. Because you are the water provider, it is essential that you provide the best water possible for your bird. Parakeets have very small bodies, and minerals and toxins will build up much more quickly in

Clean Water

It's best to change your parakeet's water twice a day. Even if you have a tube-style waterer or a product called the "two-week waterer," you must change the water daily or risk your parakeet becoming ill. Just because the package says "two-week waterer" doesn't mean that you don't have to change the water for two weeks!

Quick & Easy Parakeet Care

them than in an adult human. For this reason, it is unadvisable to use water straight from the tap as your bird's drinking water.

Tap water also contains chlorine, which can leach important nutrients from your bird's body, and your bird needs all the nutrients he can get. Bottled drinking water or filtered water is a much better option. Have a bottle of water on hand at all times for refilling your bird's dish.

Do not let your parakeet's water become dirty. Parakeets often throw things into their water, including, food, droppings, feathers, and bathing residue. You will need to change your bird's water at least twice a day. Dirty water can harbor bacteria that are potentially harmful to your bird. Your parakeet's water dishes should be clean enough for you to drink out of. Soak the water dishes in a 10-percent bleach solution once a week to sterilize them. Be sure to rinse the water dishes thoroughly before returning them to your parakeet's cage.

Seeds

Companion parakeets do well on a seed-based diet, but they can't live on seeds alone. The wild parakeet has a diet that is indeed primarily seed based, but they have one important advantage over your house parakeet: exercise. Wild parakeets fly all day long looking for food and water.

Therefore, it is important that seeds make up only a part of your parakeet's daily diet. Seeds are not bad when fed with other healthy food items as part of a

Feed your parakeet plenty of healthy foods in addition to seeds and pellets.

Fresh Seeds Only

Don't ever feed your parakeet rancid seed. If you notice an odor coming from the seeds or they feel sticky, toss them out.

balanced diet, but an all-seed diet will cause your parakeet to develop serious health issues that will shorten his life.

Wild parakeets fly many miles a day and are genetically programmed toward this kind of strenuous exercise. Your companion parakeet has the same genetic make-up, but he doesn't fly to the feeding grounds every day. Chances are that he sits near his food cup, waiting for the next meal, which may increase the likelihood that he will become overweight.

However, obesity and the health issues associated with it are easily avoided by offering your parakeet a balanced, healthful diet, and by making sure that he gets a good deal of daily exercise. If your parakeet is already tipping the scales, there are numerous things you can do to reduce his weight, such as gradually changing the bird's diet and providing more exercise. Do not delay in taking the bird to an avian veterinarian; he or she will be better able to help you devise a weight-loss plan.

How Much Seed to Feed

Even though your parakeet will relish seed, it should be offered in small amounts, making up 10 to 20 percent of your parakeet's diet. Many veterinarians suggest that people take their birds off seeds because their birds may not be getting a diet healthy enough to complement the seeds. Remember—seeds are not a bad food, but they are often misused.

A great solution is to feed your parakeet sprouted seeds, which are much higher in nutrition than dry seeds. You can find sprouted beans at the supermarket, or you can sprout seeds and beans on your own using a sprouting kit available from any health food store. Some companies sell sprouting kits for birds that you can use right out of the box.

Pellets

Pellets emerged on the bird scene a number of years ago and have quickly become a prominent trend in feeding birds. Pellets are a combination of ingredients, which the manufacturer shapes into bits that resemble seeds and other foods that birds find interesting.

As with seeds, pellets are not bad, but they are not the only food you should feed your parakeet. Variety is key. Pellets are a good base diet, but feeding them does not mean that you should exclude other foods, such as fruits, vegetables, table foods, and some seeds. Check the label on the pellets. Try to buy only all-natural, preservative-free, organic pellets. Pellets can compose 50 to 70 percent of your parakeet's total diet, with the rest consisting of other healthy foods.

Seeds vs Pellets

The seed versus pellet debate rages on in the bird community. The seed people will never touch pellets, and the pellet people feel that seed is bad. Then there are some bird keepers that feed both. Beware of the person who vehemently tells you to exclude one over the other. Seeds given in moderation are not going to kill your bird, and similarly, pellets can be a great base diet if you also offer other foods. Use your own judgment and ultimately heed the advice of your veterinarian.

Grit

It is a common myth that psittacines (parrot-type birds) need grit in their diet. In reality though, they do not. Because these birds (including your parakeet) hull their seeds, there is no need for any grit in their gizzards. Do not offer grit. It can cause a serious health problem.

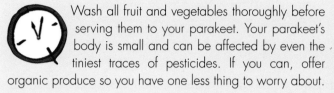

Washing Fruits and Vegetables

Wash all fruit and vegetables thoroughly before serving them to your parakeet. Your parakeet's body is small and can be affected by even the tiniest traces of pesticides. If you can, offer organic produce so you have one less thing to worry about.

Vegetables and Fruits

Feeding vegetables and fruits is a great way to give your parakeet important vitamins and minerals, and they make a fun addition to the diet. Try to feed at least four fresh vegetables or fruits a day. Eventually, you'll get to know what your parakeet's favorites are, and you can keep them on hand.

The best fruits and vegetables that you can serve are the ones that are deep green or orange in color. This type of produce has the most nutrients, especially vitamin A, which your parakeet needs to be healthy. Birds that are deficient in vitamin A are prone to respiratory problems and skin and liver problems.

Fruits and vegetables can sour quickly in warm weather, so remove them from the cage a few hours after you offer them. You can leave these foods in the cage longer in cooler weather, but make sure to take them out in the evening.

Eggs

Eggs cooked in any style are a great addition to your bird's diet. One great way to serve eggs is to boil them for about 30 minutes, cool them, and crush them, shell and all. Parakeets can eat chicken eggs if the eggs are boiled for at least 30 minutes.

Offering the fruits and vegetables is the easy part—getting your bird interested in eating them is tricky. Try chopping, grating, slicing, or offering the food whole. Clipping greens to the side of the cage is a great way to get your parakeet interested in them. Be patient. Offer new things week after week. Parakeets are curious by nature and will eventually try the new food.

Eat Your Greens

Dark-green and orange fruits and vegetables are rich in nutrients, including vitamin A, which is essential for a parakeet's health.

To get a parakeet to try new foods, you might have to "hide" them in something that the bird likes, such as muffins or omelets. If your parakeet is still fussy after a few weeks, perhaps it's because he's afraid of the dish you're using, or he's not happy with the form of the food you are offering—perhaps the food is too big or too small. Change the dishes. Cook the vegetables.

You can even bake or cook fresh veggies and fruit into breads, casseroles, and other dishes. If you are pressed for time, you can use frozen vegetables and fruits. They are not as good as their fresh counterparts, but if that's all you have time for on a particular day, go ahead. Never used canned vegetables. They contain too much salt.

Table Foods

Healthy table foods can be a wonderful addition to your parakeet's diet. With a few exceptions, your bird can eat anything and everything that you eat. Don't worry about spices—birds can eat the hottest of peppers and never flinch.

Whole-wheat and nutty-grain bread are great supplements to the bird's diet every other day, and they are especially good if you are breeding your parakeets. Whole-wheat crackers are good too, but be sure they're not too salty. Spread some peanut butter on the cracker for an extra treat.

Never indulge your bird with junk food of any kind. Salty, fatty, and sugary foods are terrible for your parakeet. Cheese is fatty, and though it's not terrible for your parakeet, birds are not equipped to digest milk products.

Toxic Foods

Birds can actually die from eating some common human foods. Never feed your parakeet chocolate, avocado, raw onions, alcohol, or fruit seeds or pits.

Bad Foods

Never feed a bird chocolate, avocado, alcohol, or caffeine, all of which can be toxic and deadly.

Vitamin and Mineral Supplements

You may have seen vitamin or mineral supplements that you add to your bird's water located in the bird section of pet shops and bird specialty shops. These pet-grade supplements will probably not harm your bird, but they probably won't do much, either. Supplements are usually only necessary for birds with special dietary needs. Consult your veterinarian before you add any supplements to your parakeet's water.

Taming and Training Your Parakeet

For most parakeet owners, being able to interact with their birds is very important. However, unless you have purchased a hand-fed baby, you can't simply take a parakeet out of the cage, place the bird on your finger, and expect him to stay and play. The parakeet will flutter or fly as far away from you as possible. So where do you begin?

The Adjustment Period

Before you can begin training your parakeet, he must fully adjust to his new home. The taming and training process will be much easier if your parakeet feels comfortable in his surroundings. Give him time to get acclimated to his new environment.

It is especially important that your bird learns to trust you during this delicate period. The key to training a parakeet—or any animal—is trust. The following are some tips that may help your bird learn to trust you.

- Talk in a soothing tone to your new bird. Say his name over and over.
- Offer treats and place them inside the cage. Let your hand linger inside the cage for a moment.
- Slowly place your hand on the side of the cage two or three times a day. Don't expect the bird to come near your finger. You're just getting him used to the look of your hand.

Even if your parakeet is already accustomed to your home and family, you can still use these tips to make training a more fun and easy experience.

Food rewards are another great way to gain the trust of parakeets. Find something he likes, such as millet spray or popcorn, and use

One way to earn the trust of your parakeet is to offer food rewards for good behaviors.

Quick & Easy Parakeet Care

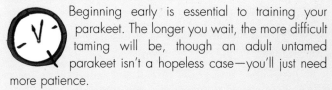
that to entice the bird to come to you. Try to tempt the bird to come to the front of the cage by holding the treat just inside the front door. Offer food whenever your parakeet has done something right, even if it's a small behavior.

Hand-Taming Your Parakeet

Once you have earned the trust of your parakeet, and you feel he has comfortably adjusted to his new home, you can begin hand-taming him. If your bird has already lived with you for some time or is already hand-tamed, the following instructions can still aid in training overall.

If you can purchase your parakeet within a few days of weaning, the taming process will be a snap. Whether you have a young bird or an older one, begin the taming process about a week to ten days after you bring your new bird home.

Wing Clipping

The first thing you need to do before you hand-tame and train your parakeet is to clip the bird's wings so that he can't fly. Don't worry; it won't hurt your parakeet, and the wing feathers will grow back.

Gentility Wins

Never use force to get your parakeet to stay on your finger or shoulder. Be gentle and soothing to instill trust, not fear.

Even if you eventually want your parakeet to be a "flyer," you will have to clip the bird during training time. Clipping a bird's wings is an easy procedure, and your avian veterinarian can show you how to do it. Do not try to clip your bird's wings without instructions from a professional.

The Taming Process

Once the bird's wings are clipped, you can begin the taming process. If your bird is untamed or semi-tame, take him out of the cage with a small towel and hold him gently in the towel to prevent him from biting you. He may struggle, but you should continue to be calm and talk to him in a low, soothing voice.

Take the bird to a small room—a bathroom is ideal, but be sure to close the toilet lid and remove any dangerous items that may fall and break if the bird comes in contact with them.

Sit on the floor with your knees bent and place the bird gently on top of your knees, holding him there for a moment before you let go. The moment you let the bird go, he will probably flutter away from you in an attempt to escape. Gather the bird again and place him on your knee once more. Repeat this action until the bird stands on your knee for a moment. Remember to remain calm. The bird may not want to stand on your knee in the first few sessions,

Bird Signals

Part of training a bird is learning all about his habits and body language. You can't tame a terrified or ill bird. A bird is best tamed when he's relaxed and content. Signs of a contented and calm bird are: preening and grooming, interest in what you're doing, a quick fluff and ruffle of the feathers, and yawning.

Hand-taming is a gradual process, but most parakeets catch on quickly and will soon allow you to handle them.

but keep trying. You can do this twice a day for 20 minutes, but no more than that. You want to begin to build trust between you and the bird, not stress him out.

Once you've gotten your bird to stand on your knee, talk to him in a very calm voice and begin to move one hand slowly up your leg toward the bird. This may cause the bird to flutter off your knee again. No matter—simply try again.

Be Patient
Little by little, session after session, move your hand slowly up your leg until the bird allows it to come very close. The idea here is that the bird should eventually allow contact with your hand. This may take quite a while, so be patient.

Handle With Care

Using gloves during training sessions isn't a good idea. Not only will they terrify your parakeet, they will get the bird used to the gloves, not your bare hand. Be brave and withstand a few nips!

Once the bird allows your hand to approach closely, try to tickle his chest with your finger or scratch his head and neck if he allows. After a few sessions of doing this, you can try to get the bird to stand on your hand.

At the end of the training session, place your parakeet back in the cage. Give him a treat and tell him what a good bird he is. After a few moments, you can allow him out for independent playtime. It is important for your parakeet to feel that training is an enjoyable experience.

If your bird is young and not a biter, you can place him on your finger and sit in a small, safe room with him, talking to him in a low, soothing voice. Put him on your shoulder while you watch television. The bird will soon realize that it's fun to interact with you, and you can then move on to more advanced training.

Training Your Parakeet

There are many fun things you can train your parakeet to do, but the first and most important command you should teach your parakeet is the "Step-Up" command.

Teaching the "Step-Up" Command

"Step up" is the act of your bird stepping onto your hand or finger, without hesitation. Parakeets are not hatched knowing how to do this; they must be taught. Perhaps your parakeet came to you already hand trained—great! But it is still important to reinforce the step-up command so that it becomes second nature to your bird.

Assuming that you are teaching a tame or semi-tame parakeet the step-up command, begin by allowing the bird to come out of the cage on his own. You win nothing by fishing the bird out, and you will only succeed in beginning your training session on a bad note.

The step-up command is one of the most important lessons you can teach your parakeet.

Place a perch on top of the parakeet's cage, or let the bird climb onto a perch where he will be standing on a dowel, not a flat surface. If your parakeet is a tame youngster, you can gently lift him out of the cage, but because he doesn't yet know how to step up, be careful not to pull too hard on his feet. He will grip the perch because he doesn't understand what you want from him.

Once the bird is out, give him a treat. This will show him that training sessions can be fun, and he will look forward to them. Making training sessions fun is extremely important and will earn your further trust from your parakeet.

Next, begin rubbing the bird's chest and belly softly and gently with the length of your index finger, cooing to him, and slowly increasing the pressure with which you push on his belly. This can go on for days, depending on the tameness of your bird. Your semi-tame bird may not be sure what you are up to, and he might be wary of this stroking. Take things slowly, and work to gain your parakeet's trust. A tamer bird will often sit there, enjoying the attention.

As the training sessions continue, increase the pressure on the belly—pushing slightly on a bird's chest will put the bird off balance, and he will lift a foot up to right himself. Place your finger or hand under the foot and lift him, if he allows. If not, simply allow the bird's foot to remain on your hand until he removes it. As you do this, tell the bird to "Step up."

You must always say, "Step up" when the bird steps onto your hand. It is essential that the bird associate the action with the phrase. Many parakeets will eventually say, "Step up" themselves and wave one foot in the air when they want you to pick them up. This becomes a great communication tool.

This parakeet enjoys playing with her toys.

Quick & Easy Parakeet Care

Talking

Attempting to talk is a parakeet's way of communicating with you and learning your language. Talking indicates a deep affection (or at least a heightened attentiveness) for a parakeet's owners. The more attention and affection you lavish on your parakeet, the more likely he is to talk to you.

Training Do's and Don'ts

Do's

- Do bribe your parakeet with fun foods and toys he likes.

- Do move slowly and talk in a soothing manner.

- Do try to read your parakeet's body language—if the bird is becoming terrified or frustrated, put him in the cage for a rest.

- Do several short training sessions a day rather than one or two long ones.

- Do have realistic expectations for your parakeet. Training takes time.

Don'ts

- Don't grab a frightened bird out of the cage and whisk him away to another room. This can be traumatizing.

- Don't wear gloves during taming or training. Gloves will only terrify your parakeet, and he won't get used to the human hand.

- Don't yell at or hit your parakeet, ever. It is not a good training tactic and is considered animal abuse.

- Don't get your feelings hurt if you get bitten. A bite isn't personal. The bird is just being a bird.

- Don't tire the bird. Training sessions should last between 15 and 25 minutes.

Biting is sometimes unavoidable during training, but don't scold your bird or punish him—it is natural for your parakeet to act this way in the beginning.

Biting

Biting is sometimes unavoidable when hand-taming and training a parakeet, especially if you are trying to tame an older bird. A younger bird doesn't have much of a bite—sure, it hurts a bit, but it doesn't generally draw blood.

Remember to never hit or shout at a bird that's biting you. This is simply going to provoke more biting and mistrust. The more of a reaction that you give when the bird bites you, the more frequently and the harder the bird is going to bite.

Say It Like You Mean It

Words and phrases said with energy behind them are interesting to your parakeet. This is why greetings, names, commands, and curses seem easier for a bird to learn.

However, if you're calm and act as if the bite doesn't hurt a bit, the bird will be less likely to bite the next time. The bird is biting to get you away from him—and this works, almost without fail. You get bitten and you put the bird away—that's what he wants. Don't let him train you this way. If you are consistent and patient when working with your bird, in time, the bad behaviors will stop.

Most parakeets love talking and can learn hundreds of words and phrases.

Teaching Your Parakeet to Talk

Parakeets are among the best talkers in the parrot family and are able to learn hundreds of words and phrases. Teaching your parakeet to talk is fairly easy, but it can take some time. Some gifted parakeets will learn to talk in just a few weeks, while others may not talk for a year.

The first attempts at talking will sound like garbled English. This is "baby talk." Once baby talk begins, you'll start to hear the words become clearer. This is the time to correct pronunciation, repeating the phrases that the bird is attempting (if you understand them) back to him, the way they should sound. You'll be surprised at how clearly your parakeet will begin to repeat the words if you teach him how they're meant to be said.

Pairs will be less likely to talk than the single bird, and single birds with mirrors will be less likely to talk than single birds without mirrors. If a parakeet has something to talk to, he may not talk to you. If you want more than one bird but still want to teach your first bird to talk, wait until your bird is talking and then get him a friend to pal around with.

Pairs of parakeets may talk less often than single parakeets, but it is beneficial to the birds to have the constant attention of a mate.

If you want your parakeet to talk, don't teach him to whistle first. Whistling is easier and apparently more fun than talking, and is often preferred by the bird. You can teach your bird to excel at whistling after he has learned several phrases.

Teaching a parakeet to talk is all about repetition. The more you repeat a word or phrase, the more likely your parakeet is to learn it. A parakeet has to hear a word or phrase over and over many times before he masters it. Once you've decided on a phrase you want your bird to learn, say it over and over every time you pass the cage, and be sure to say it clearly.

Grooming Your Parakeet

Parakeets, like many companion birds, do not require much in the way of grooming. However, some maintenance is necessary, such as occasional toenail clipping and baths, and some owners choose to clip the wings on their parakeets.

Wing Clipping

To prevent a bird from flying, some people cut the lower half of the primary flight feathers (the first ten feathers) off of both of the wings. This practice is common among pet owners and is a painless procedure, much like getting a haircut. Like hair, however, the flight feathers do grow back in about five to six months or after a molt. If you want to keep your parakeet's wings clipped, check the flight feathers every month or so to make sure none have grown out.

Wing Clipping—Pros and Cons

Wing clipping is a very controversial topic among bird enthusiasts and pet owners.

When clipped, your parakeet will not be able to fly away and get lost if you or someone in your household carelessly opens a window or a door, though a clipped bird has no defense against predators in the home, like the family dog or cat.

A home is not a safe place for a bird to fly either. There are many dangers in a home, including mirrors and closed windows, standing water, and toxic substances that an unclipped bird can find more easily than a clipped bird.

However, because it's not very safe for a bird to have full flight in a home, many believe that owners should build his or her parakeets a flight cage or an aviary so that they can have full flight.

Many parakeet owners do build aviaries and habitats for their birds. This is a great way to allow your birds to fly and get their much-needed exercise. Flying is indeed a wonderful psychological and

Clipping the Wings

Learn to clip your parakeet by watching someone experienced in clipping, like an avian veterinarian, a breeder, or a bird shop owner. Often, you won't even have to clip your bird yourself. If you can find someone in your area who will charge you just a few dollars for clipping, it might just be worth the cost.

physical experience for birds. It might be a good idea to consider providing an aviary or habitat for your parakeet before making the decision to clip his wings.

How Much To Clip

Clipping should allow your parakeet to flutter gently to the floor. If you cut too much, there is the potential for injury. If you cut too little, the bird could take off into the wild blue yonder.

How to Clip Your Parakeet's Wings

Clipping a parakeet is a job for two people. One person needs to hold the parakeet gently in a small hand towel, and one person has to clip the wings. The person clipping the wings should extend the wing carefully, exposing the individual feathers.

You will see the primary flight feathers at the end of the wing, with shorter feathers, the coverts, covering the upper part of the flights— don't cut these feathers! Cut the flight feathers parallel to the coverts, about two millimeters away from them. Never cut into a feather inside a sheath—this is a "living" feather, and it will bleed.

Blood feathers, also called pinfeathers, are newly grown feathers that still have a blood supply. Recognize blood feathers by the sheath of material encasing them. If your parakeet is light in color, you may even be able to see a vein inside the feather. Trim feathers in a clean, well-lighted place, and keep styptic powder on hand in case you accidentally clip a blood feather. Take the bird to an avian veterinarian should bleeding occur. As an alternative, you can pull the bleeding feather out firmly but gently from the root; however, leaving it inside the wing can cause infection. Be careful!

Trim the feathers on both wings evenly. Don't trim only one wing. This does not allow the parakeet to control descent, and he could

If you do decide to clip your parakeet's wings, make sure you have a professional take on this task or show you how to do it first.

easily injure himself when trying to land. Some people will advise you to leave the first two primary flight feathers intact, but this is not a recommended practice; your parakeet could break these feathers easily because the other feathers on the wing no longer protect them.

Toenail Clipping

Your parakeet may develop sharp toenails, which will make your interactions with him unpleasant. Even though your parakeet might have a concrete perch, which is great for keeping the nails trimmed, you might have to trim the nails as well.

The nail has two parts, just like our nails do—the dead part of the nail (on the end) and the quick, where the blood supply is. Cut the dead part of the nail, never the quick. This is easy when you have a parakeet with light-colored nails—you'll be able to see the vein in the nail and avoid it. If you have a bird with dark-colored nails, simply trim a very tiny amount off the tip of the nail, rather than risk hurting your bird.

Quick & Easy Parakeet Care

Again, as with wing trimming, you will have to gather your parakeet up in a hand towel. A nail trimmer for humans works well for your parakeet's little nails. Keep styptic powder on hand at all times when you trim your bird's toenails in case of bleeding. Better yet, have a professional do it for you.

If your parakeet's nails become sharp and are not filed down naturally by concrete perches or other rough surfaces, you may have to trim them.

Instead of clipping, make a few passes at your parakeet's nails with a file once a week—this will keep the nails trim and will eliminate the chances of hurting your bird. With both toes and wings, it's better to clip less than a lot—you can always go back and clip more, but you can't take away the fact that you've cut into a blood feather or the quick of a nail.

The Dangers of Beak Grooming

Most veterinarians recommend that owners do not trim their bird's beak. If your parakeet's beak seems overgrown, the bird may have a serious health disorder that needs to be addressed by a veterinarian. The doctor can help your bird with the health problem and trim the beak at the same time. A healthy bird does things with his beak that will naturally wear it down, such as eating hard foods, playing with toys, wiping his beak on perches, and chewing on wood. There is a problem if your parakeet's beak needs trimming.

Bathing

Parakeets love to bathe, and it's a real treat to watch them happily splashing away in a birdbath. There are many kinds of birdbaths on the market, and no one type is superior to another. There's a shallow type of bath that hangs on the outside of the cage and allows the bird to enter and splash around with a minimal amount of water spilled outside of the cage. There are also types with a mirror on the bottom that seem to be quite popular.

Parakeets love to bathe, so it's a good idea to purchase a birdbath for your pet; you can also use a mister or spray bottle to bathe him.

Many parakeet owners use misters or spray bottles to bathe their birds. Remember to use tepid to warm water and encourage bathing in the daylight hours so that the bird doesn't go to sleep wet.

Bath Time!

Bathing is important for a bird's skin and feather health. Dry skin can cause itching and can lead to feather plucking.

You might not think that bathing in winter is a good idea, but your bird might insist on it! Your home may be very dry in winter, and he may need to moisten his skin. Birds generally know what's best when it comes to bathing, so trust their instincts. There's no need to blow-dry or towel dry your parakeet unless your home is cold and you can't provide your parakeet with a warm lamp under which to dry himself. If you choose to blow-dry your bird, do so on the lowest setting, and make sure the air is not too warm. Only a tolerant bird will allow blow-drying.

Quick & Easy Parakeet Care

Parakeet Health Care

Birds are great at hiding their illnesses until the illness becomes quite advanced. A bird in the wild that shows symptoms of illness is a target for predators. Through millions of years of evolution, birds have learned to behave as if they are perfectly well even when they aren't. Unfortunately, this pretense is not helpful in diagnosing a problem in its initial stages.

The best way to recognize symptoms that could indicate illness is to pay close attention to your parakeet's normal behaviors and daily habits. Every parakeet is an individual, and some traits that are abnormal in one bird may be perfectly normal in another. However, if you notice activity or changes from your bird's

Pay close attention to your bird's normal routine so that you can recognize any changes that could indicate illness.

normal routine, it's best to take your parakeet to an avian veterinarian.

Choosing an Avian Veterinarian

An avian veterinarian specializes in the care and treatment of birds. Birds are quite different from dogs and cats and need a special doctor trained in the particular treatment of bird accidents, ailments, and diseases. A veterinarian that specializes in birds is likely to catch a subtle symptom of illness and will mostly likely perform the most suitable tests when necessary. It's best to take your parakeet for checkups at least once a year anyway, even if you don't notice anything out of the ordinary.

The Initial Visit

You should take your new pet to an avian veterinarian within three days of buying him. The following are good reasons for doing that:

• If you bought your parakeet with a health guarantee, you will have some recourse if tests reveal that your new bird is ill.

- You will begin a relationship with the avian veterinarian. This doctor will get to know your bird and be able to evaluate him better because he or she will have a "healthy reference."
- Some avian veterinarians will not take an emergency patient unless the bird is a regular patient.
- Avian veterinarians often board birds in their offices, but some will only board patients. This way, he or she can be relatively sure that the bird will not bring diseases into his or her office.
- You will receive important recommendations from the doctor, including information on diet and housing.

Signs and Symptoms of a Sick Parakeet

It's important to know the signs and symptoms of illness that may require a trip to his avian veterinarian. If your parakeet usually greets you when you come home from work with a concert of whistles or an explosion of jabbering and talking, and one day that doesn't happen, you can be sure that something is going on with your bird.

An avian veterinarian is the only individual who should diagnose and treat your parakeet for illness.

Fluffiness

If you notice that your parakeet is fluffed up for an extended amount of time, he may be trying to retain heat.

Sleeping Too Much

A parakeet that is sick may sleep too much. Sleeping on the bottom of the cage could also be a sign of illness.

Loss of Appetite

You should know how much and what types of food your parakeet is consuming each day. If you notice that your bird is not eating, there could be a problem.

Attitude Change

If your parakeet seems listless and is not behaving in his usual manner, he might be ill.

Lameness

If your bird can't use his feet, there is definitely a problem.

Panting or Labored Breathing

Either of these symptoms can indicate a respiratory ailment or overheating.

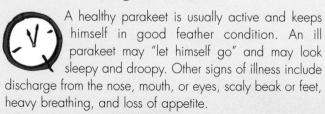

Signs of Illness

A healthy parakeet is usually active and keeps himself in good feather condition. An ill parakeet may "let himself go" and may look sleepy and droopy. Other signs of illness include discharge from the nose, mouth, or eyes, scaly beak or feet, heavy breathing, and loss of appetite.

Discharge

If you notice any runniness or discharge from the eyes, nostrils, or vent, take the bird to the veterinarian immediately.

Food Stuck to the Feathers Around the Face

This indicates poor grooming or regurgitation. Both are possible signs of illness.

Changes in Droppings

Your parakeet's droppings should consist of a solid green portion, white urates (on top of

A healthy parakeet is active and keeps her feathers in good condition.

the green), and a clear liquid. If any of these are discolored (black, yellow, or red) and there has been no change in diet, there might be a problem.

Common Parakeet Ailments

Parakeets are prone to several diseases and ailments, many of which are preventable. The following section outlines many of these ailments. However, make sure to use this information as a guide only. Your avian veterinarian is the only person who should actually treat these ailments.

Self-Mutilation

Parakeets that have physical or psychological disorders may pick and chew their feathers. If the problem is medical or nutritional, an avian veterinarian may help solve the problem. If the problem is psychological, you may have to be more diligent in caring for your bird and keeping it happy. Birds that are confined or kept in stressful situations may pick themselves in order to relieve the stress or boredom. Provide your bird with enough space and toys, and of course, a trip to the veterinarian.

Providing your parakeet with enough space, toys, and attention should prevent most behavior problems.

Mites

Scaly-face mites, or *Knemidokoptes* mites, occur in young parakeets and older birds with compromised immune systems. These mites cause a crusty appearance on the bird's face and legs and can result in an overgrown beak. They are easy to treat but require multiple treatments to eliminate them completely. Scaly-face mites are not very contagious but can be passed from bird to bird.

The tiny feather mite is not common in parakeets, but it can infest birds that live outdoors in unclean conditions. Red mites eat their host's blood and are highly contagious, though not very common in parakeets. If you suspect mites, do not try to get rid of them yourself—see the avian veterinarian.

Giardia

Giardia is a one-celled protozoan that can affect your parakeet and can also affect other people and animals in the house. Giardia is passed through contaminated food or water and affects the digestive tract. You may notice diarrhea, itching, an inability to digest foods, weight loss, and other symptoms. Have your veterinarian test for this parasite.

Worms

Roundworms are commonly found in parakeets; for this reason, your vet should test for them during your bird's first veterinary visit. If roundworms are found, routine tests and treatments should be performed on the bird because eliminating these worms can sometimes take years.

Keeping your parakeet's environment clean and dry will help prevent fungal infections, such as Aspergillosis.

Aspergillosis

Aspergillosis is a fungal infection that causes respiratory distress and can be deadly. Any changes in your parakeet's breathing, changes in vocalization, or gasping and wheezing can indicate this infection. Aspergillosis is diagnosable by your avian veterinarian, but it's difficult to treat and may take months of medication and treatment. Keeping your parakeet's environment very clean and dry will help prevent this infection.

Yeast

Yeast infections, or candidasis, affects the mouth, digestive tract,

Nutritious Foods

Offering your parakeet foods that are loaded with vitamin A, such as green leafy vegetables and orange fruits and vegetables, can help prevent yeast infections—just make sure that your bird actually eats them.

and can involve the respiratory system. Your parakeet normally has a certain amount of yeast in his body, but when his bodily balance is upset, as when the bird is undernourished or after a treatment of antibiotics, the fungus yeast can grow to excess.

A parakeet with yeast will have a sticky substance in his mouth and may have white mouth lesions. Regurgitation and digestive problems may occur. Treatment by a veterinarian is necessary. Even though this condition is not immediately serious, it can cause death if left untreated.

Tuberculosis

Mycobacterium avium is responsible for the tuberculosis infection and can be transmitted in food, water, or by filthy cage parts. Avian tuberculosis can be transmitted to humans with compromised immune systems, so the caretaker must be careful to avoid infection. While tuberculosis in humans is a respiratory disease, it is primarily a digestive disorder in parakeets. Symptoms include weight loss and digestive disorders.

Make sure your veterinarian tests your bird for psittacosis (parrot fever) and polyoma virus.

Psittacosis (Parrot Fever)

Psittacosis, also called chlamydiosis and parrot fever, is also transmittable to humans and causes respiratory distress symptoms in both humans and birds. Psittacosis is transmitted through droppings and infected secretions. Some parakeets can be carriers of the disease without showing any symptoms. Ask your veterinarian to test for this disease, especially if there's someone with a weakened immune system in contact with your parakeet.

Quick & Easy Parakeet Care

Better Breathing

Birds are prone to respiratory illness and distress because their respiratory system is more complicated than ours. If you notice that your parakeet is panting, call your avian veterinarian immediately. Always keep your parakeet away from fumes and airborne toxins in order to prevent unnecessary respiratory distress.

Megabacteria

Megabacteria are large bacteria found in parts of the parakeet's digestive system. These bacteria cause disease in parakeets, but not much is known about this condition at this time. Diagnosis generally occurs after death. It goes without saying that keeping your parakeet healthy with the proper nutrition and routine veterinary care will go a long way in preventing disease.

Psittacine Beak and Feather Disease

PBFD is an incurable, contagious (to other birds) disease that involves feather loss and beak lesions in the later stages of the disease. Diagnosis is through a blood test, and euthanasia is generally recommended because this disease is fatal. Symptoms include feather loss, abnormal feather growth, and a generally ill condition.

Polyoma Virus

Polyoma virus usually affects young parakeets, though adult birds are carriers. Adult birds transmit the disease to their young, and they die around the time of fledging. This disease occurs mainly among breeding stock, though households with many birds are susceptible as well, especially if you plan to add young birds to the household.

There is no treatment for polyoma virus, so prevention is essential. Make sure to have your avian veterinarian test all of your parakeets for this disease.

Pacheco's Disease

Pacheco's disease is a viral hepatitis that affects the liver. This disease is fatal and is mainly diagnosed upon death, which comes rapidly. This is a highly contagious disease that can be transmitted easily when you bring a new bird into your home, so always enforce strict quarantine by separating a new bird from your other birds during the first month after being brought into your home.

Regular veterinary checkups can help prevent reproductive disorders in breeding pairs.

Reproductive Disorders

An undernourished egg-laying hen, especially one that hasn't gotten enough calcium in her diet, may have eggs with soft shells that will be difficult to lay, resulting in egg binding.

This can also occur when the egg is malformed, or if she has a tumor or other disorder of the reproductive system. Some symptoms of egg binding include panting and lameness. Keeping the laying hen fit and nourished will help prevent this problem. Consult your veterinarian immediately if you suspect that your bird is suffering from this reproductive disorder.

Older male parakeets may develop tumors on the testicles (located inside their body) and, consequently, the ceres may change colors. Regular veterinary checkups should help to find and treat any developing problems like this.

Gout

Gout is a painful condition of the legs common in parakeets that

Provide your parakeets with spacious living quarters and plenty of activities so that they will get enough exercise.

don't get the proper nutrition. Symptoms include visible swellings on the legs and subsequent lameness.

Bumblefoot
Bumblefoot is an infection of the bottom of the feet and is associated with poor nutrition and obesity. The skin on the bottom of the foot may be inflamed, red, and may become scabby, resulting in lameness.

Lameness
Lameness and weakness in the feet is sometimes associated with hens that are egg bound, but there can be multiple reasons for this, including tumors. See your avian veterinarian if you notice any foot or leg weakness.

Fun Toys

Parakeets like to chew, and the more they chew, the more energy they are expending. Find toys that your bird likes to fight with and chew. He will get more exercise that way.

Parakeet Health Care

Healthy Exercise

Parakeets are active birds in general, but they can become obese if kept in a cage that is too small. Provide spacious living quarters and allow your bird to have time out of his cage daily. The best exercise is to simply let your bird out of the cage to play with you. The more out-of-cage time that your parakeet has, the more exercise he will get, and the healthier and happier he will be. Some people allow their parakeets to walk along the floor for exercise, but it's best not to do this. This is a dangerous practice because the bird is in the perfect position to be stepped on or crushed.

Many people build aviaries where their birds can fly. Flying is the best exercise for birds. It's the most natural form of exercise and also gives them a sense of purpose. Some people allow their parakeets to fly around the house. However, be aware that there are many dangers lurking in the household, and flying in the house may not be the best idea. If you do let your bird fly around the house, keep a close eye on him and keep him out of trouble.

Resources

ORGANIZATIONS

American Federation of Aviculture, Inc.
P.O. Box 7312
N. Kansas City, MO 64116
Telephone: (816) 421-2473
Fax: (816) 421-3214
E-mail: afaoffice@aol.com
www.AFAbirds.org

Avicultural Society of America
Secretary: Helen Hanson
E-mail: info@asabirds.org
www.asabirds.org

Budgerigar Association of America
Secretary: Kerry Laverty
E-mail: pro@applink.net
www.budgerigarassociation.com

The American Budgerigar Society
Secretary: Diane Ingram
E-mail: abssecretary@cs.com
www.abs1.org

PUBLICATIONS

Bird Talk Magazine
3 Burroughs
Irvine, CA 92618
Telephone: (949) 855-8822
Fax: (949) 855-3045
www.animalnetwork.com/birdtalk/defa
ult.asp

Budgerigar World
E-mail: budgerigarworld@msn.com
www.budgerigarworld.com

Winged Wisdom Magazine
Birds n Ways

39760 Calle Bellagio
Temecula, CA 92592
Telephone: (909) 303-9376
www.birdsnways.com

INTERNET RESOURCES

Budgerigars Galore
(www.budgerigars.co.uk)
Budgerigars Galore offers a variety of
information on topics like nutrition,
breeding, and health. The site also
provides tips for beginners and links to
other budgie pages.

VETERINARY RESOURCES

Association of Avian Veterinarians
(AAV)
P.O. Box 811720
Boca Raton, FL 33481-1720
Telephone: (561) 393-8901
Fax: (561) 393-8902
E-mail: AAVCTRLOFC@aol.com
www.aav.org

EMERGENCY RESOURCES AND RESCUE ORGANIZATIONS

ASPCA Animal Poison Control Center
Telephone: (888) 426-4435
E-mail: napcc@aspca.org (for non-
emergency, general information only)
www.apcc.aspca.org

Bird Hotline
P.O. Box 1411
Sedona, AZ 86339-1411
E-mail: birdhotline@birdhotline.com
www.birdhotline.com

Index

Photo Credits

Joan Balzarini: 42
Susan Chamberlain: 21
Isabelle Francais: 50, 53
Michael Gilroy: 5, 9, 11, 15, 17, 57, 61
Eric Ilasenko: 33

Bonnie Jay: 3, 4, 13, 34, 37, 45, 56
Mary Ann Kahn: 40, 52
Robert Pearcy: 10, 51
Lara Stern: 8, 55
John Tyson: 43, 44

Quick & Easy Parakeet Care